FAIRACRES PUBLIC.

AN ECOLOGY OF THE HEART

FAITH THROUGH THE CLIMATE CRISIS

DUNCAN FORBES

SLG Press

© 2023 SLG Press
First Edition 2023

Fairacres Publications No. 201

Print ISBN 978-0-7283-0353-9
Fairacres Publications Series ISSN 0307-1405

The publishers have no control over, or responsibility for, any third-party website referred to in this book. All internet addresses given in this book were correct at the time of going to press. The authors and publisher regret any inconvenience caused if addresses have changed or sites have ceased to exist, but can accept no responsibility for any such changes.

Edited and typeset in Palatino Linotype by Julia Craig-McFeely

Biblical quotations are taken from the New Revised Standard Version of the Bible unless otherwise noted

SLG Press
Convent of the Incarnation
Fairacres • Oxford
www.slgpress.co.uk

Printed by
Grosvenor Group Ltd, Loughton, Essex

CONTENTS

AN ECOLOGY OF THE HEART

1
INTRODUCTION
THE PROBLEM

Terms such as 'climate grief' and 'ecological anxiety' are now becoming well recognized. They describe the sadness and desolation triggered in many people in response to the recognition of the losses taking place, and ones that are predicted as a result of our changing climate. We know that, everywhere, what we call the 'natural world' is not as it was. We know that sea level rises are already built-in to our future, and that Pacific island communities and many major cities will probably be inundated at some point. We know that dangerous weather events from extreme cold, hurricanes and floods to life-threatening heatwaves and droughts, are occurring more frequently, bringing with them untold suffering. For those in much of Europe such large-scale happenings may still seem remote, but in our own localities we are aware of the huge reduction in the number of bees, butterflies and moths. How often in the South of England is the cuckoo now heard? Each spring we look out anxiously for the returning swifts, conscious that their tremendous migratory journeys are becoming ever more perilous.

Many of us experience 'climate grief', a kind of low-level, background sadness, fluctuating in intensity from day to day but always there. It is, I imagine, similar to the settled state of bereavement that is felt after someone who was dearly loved has died and the immediate and acute pangs of loss have dulled a little, or to the anticipatory grief of being alongside a dear friend treading a slow pathway towards death from a terminal disease. There are indeed good days, times when it seems possible to live in the moment, to be lost in the simplicity of being alive, the joy of beauty or the love of others. But what we often designate as reality invariably breaks back in and we feel, yet again, that those moments of happiness are but borrowed time. The stream of sadness deep within the heart flows on, sometimes in spate when anxieties become acute, sometimes more quietly, but never entirely ceasing.

What are we to do with this aching that is sometimes dull, sometimes sharp? Whilst it cannot compare with what many millions are already experiencing directly from a chaotic climate, we now see that nowhere is immune from extreme weather events, from real physical suffering and even death. We are finally realizing that any of us may become victims soon. How should we react to this? What insights might we gain from the world's faith traditions, particularly Christianity? These are old questions, ones with which every generation wrestles; questions of what, if any, meaning can be found in the seemingly-random disasters that befall us. They are questions that are central to every religious account of the world, from the most crude to the most sophisticated and, in the absence of any conclusively satisfactory answer, they continue to be asked. What follows in this book are some reflections that have arisen from an attempt to look honestly both at the extent of the ecological crises that humanity faces, and at the new and searching questions that these put to faith.

I start by considering climate change as an existential threat, given the current scientific forecasts, and proceed to examine the implications of that threat to our individual and collective sense of identity and security, drawing on the sociological work of Peter Berger. This examination underlines the importance of the narratives, or stories, that we hold in common for our individual and social wellbeing, and how threatening it can feel if these stories start to unravel. In that context I examine how responses to the trauma of a diagnosis of terminal illness can shed useful light on our reactions to the anticipated or actual trauma of climate change, especially in relation to the seeking and adoption of new narratives. I consider the ways in which climate change challenges our faith-narratives, specifically the traditional Christian portrayals of the pivotal role of human beings in God's purpose for the cosmos and earth. I suggest revised accounts of the human place in Creation and examine the importance of lament in social adaptation and resilience during times of challenge and change. I conclude with reflections on what we might learn from the Christian contemplative tradition about living in this new era of uncertainty.

This examination has both a pastoral and a practical aim: pastoral responses to climate anxieties are in their infancy, so if they are to be effective they will require an awareness of the ways in which such anxiety may differ from other kinds of emotional distress. Practically, it is often said that taking action can provide a sense of purpose and thus improve individual wellbeing. Similarly, addressing deep-seated anxieties, and perhaps even the possibility of panic, in informed and responsible ways can free individuals for constructive action.

I am very conscious that there is no 'view from nowhere'. Every perspective is prejudiced by the standpoint of the viewer, and by the influences acting on their view. These influences may be from a cultural and social context, from personal experience, the existence of idiosyncratic blind spots, or factors in our immediate circumstances or environment. The approach taken here is thus inescapably partial. Nonetheless it is offered in the hope that it can contribute in some small way to the fundamental changes in perception, and the consequential action, that will be essential if humanity is to survive the coming storms.

Some of the terms I use may be unfamiliar. We recognize terms describing geological epochs during which the planet went through phases of development that affected its ecology, particularly global climatic events, the extinction of some animal forms and the emergence of Homo sapiens as the dominant species. The term 'Anthropocene', originating in the Earth Sciences, has been widely adopted to refer to the present era of geological time because human activity is now considered to be the dominant influence shaping the environment, climate, and ecology of the earth.[1] It has been widely adopted across academia and the public sphere as a catch-all description for the overwhelming impact of human activity on the planet.[2] While many, therefore, continue to look to outside forces as those that define a geological era, scientists and lay people alike are increasingly beginning to understand that we can no longer ignore our own influence as the cause of the defining planetary changes that we are experiencing.

This means that the terms of reference defining our relationship with our world are no longer what we thought they were. The term 'nomos' was coined by Peter Berger in his classic work, *The Sacred Canopy*, published over thirty years ago, to denote the meaningful order that is maintained for us by the narratives about the world that we hold in common.[3] In particular he refers to the specific sense of the ordering of the world and experience by human societies that provide coherence, meaning and stability to social life. One of Berger's primary claims is that the generation and sustaining of a nomos is vital

---

[1] It was included in the *Oxford English Dictionary* in 2014, and is now well established.

[2] See the *Open Encyclopedia of Anthropology* (formerly the *Cambridge Encyclopedia of Anthropology*). This resource is only available online at: www.anthroencyclopedia.com/entry/anthropocene, accessed 25 April 2023.

[3] Peter L. Berger, *The Sacred Canopy: Elements of a Sociological Theory of Religion* (Anchor Books, 1990).

to enable people to cope with what would otherwise be an intolerable awareness of human insignificance and mortality, and the haunting threat of the ultimate futility of life:

> The socially established nomos may thus be understood, perhaps in its most important aspect, as a shield against terror. Put differently, the most important function of society is nomization … Men are congenitally compelled to impose a meaningful order upon reality. This order, however, presupposes the social enterprise of ordering world-construction.[4]

Although much writing within a Christian context still refers to the Old and New Testaments, a more recent practice, one I have adopted here, is to speak respectively of the Tanakh and the Messianic Writings. This honours Judaism and is a reminder of how the Christian approach to Scripture can be distorted by supersessionism.

One of the emphases in my argument is the unknowability of the Absolute. How then to refer to that of which we cannot speak, that is, 'God'? Jean-Luc Marion in his influential book *God Without Being* crossed out the vowel when he wanted to indicate the inadequacy of all concepts of the Divine.[5] Timothy Gorringe in *Keeping Time* uses 'G-d' with the same intention.[6] I have kept to the traditional form, on the assumption that readers will be alive to the provisional nature of any concept of the Ultimate.

For convenience I use the well-recognized phrase 'climate change' as a kind of shorthand for the multiple and interrelated threats to our planet. The immediate cause of our rapidly changing climate is the extraction and burning of fossil fuels

---

[4] Berger, *The Sacred Canopy*, 22.

[5] Jean-Luc Marion, *God Without Being* (University of Chicago Press, 2nd Edition 2012), 105.

[6] Timothy Gorringe, *Keeping Time: Time, Liturgy and Christian Discipleship* (Sacristy Press, 2022), viii.

which has taken place at an ever-accelerating rate for 250 years. Behind that is the Western materialistic lifestyle spreading round the globe, itself inseparable from an economic model that assumes endless growth on a finite planet. It can do this because 'natural capital' — what all life ultimately depends upon hour-by-hour for its continuing survival — is afforded no value on the balance-sheets of global corporations, and but little on those of many governments. The guardians of natural capital, the indigenous peoples and the cultures and wisdoms of earlier ways of life than our own, have been lost or marginalized, many of them victims of colonial ideology and its extractive propensities. 'Climate change' as used here goes beyond rising temperatures and extreme weather events: under its shadow are also mass extinctions, ecological degradation on land and in the seas, climate-related migrations of people, the spread of disease, and many of the acute political issues of our time that are exacerbated by a hostile climate, including poverty and social injustice.

2
ASSESSING THE EVIDENCE

Engagement with emotional, pastoral and theological issues arising from an anticipated dire future requires some awareness of the scientific consensus and an individual judgement about the severity of what may be coming. Both for our own mental equilibrium and to guide us in our actions, it is important to be rigorous in assessing the evidence, otherwise, depending on our personalities, we may allow our negative feelings to run beyond the science or relax into an unjustifiable optimism. So how serious *are* the multiple and interlocking crises now threatening the world? This fundamental question is, unfortunately, impossible to answer with certainty. We just do not know, and cannot know, precisely what the future holds for our own lives, let alone for our planet. Views ranging from extreme pessimism to a confident optimism are promulgated via multiple media.

The story of how human life has changed the planet is not a new one. Even the definition of the term 'Anthropocene' is still contested, with argument continuing over the date it was first used. It is undeniably the case that for thousands of years humans have affected other living beings as well as the atmosphere through forest clearance, agriculture and in many other ways. However, since about the middle of the eighteenth century the impact of such activities has expanded and accelerated dramatically. We are now at the point, or perhaps past it, where the natural equilibrium of the earth's systems cannot be depended upon. We can no longer be confident of the capacity of the earth to absorb and adjust, gradually and benignly, to the consequences of current human ways of living.[7] Increasing numbers of extreme weather events are giving us early warning of the likelihood of worse to come.

For the first time in history the future of the whole planet is in human hands, and depends upon the decisions that are taken, or fail to be taken, in the next few decades. The consequences, for good or ill, of the choices we make as a species will determine the future of the earth for millennia or even for millions of years. This is an awesome responsibility and requires a fundamental reorientation in our relationships with the multiple interrelated systems that enable life—with all that is encompassed in what we call the environment. The situation in which we now find ourselves also calls into question many of the old ways in which we have envisaged humanity's place in the world and the meaning of our lives, traditionally the preserve of religion. The question whether and how faith responds and adapts to these challenges is a vital one.

In this context, might the future really be 'worse, much worse, than you think', as David Wallace-Wells stated in the opening sentence of *The Uninhabitable Earth*?[8] Although this claim was strongly contested in certain quarters, it shows the gap that Wallace-Wells had identified between what he saw as the scientific consensus and the complacency of much of Western society. His work followed that of Professor Jem Bendell, who took a year's sabbatical to examine for himself the scientific consensus on climate change and ecological collapse. This led to his highly-influential paper 'Deep Adaptation' of 2018, revised in 2020, in which Bendell concludes that future disruption will be so extensive that it will lead to social

---

[7] For a useful overview see Erle C. Ellis, *Anthropocene: A Very Short Introduction* (Oxford University Press, 2018).
[8] David Wallace-Wells, *The Uninhabitable Earth: A Story of the Future* (Penguin, 2019).

breakdown.[9] His pessimism — or perhaps realism — is echoed by former journalist Dahr Jamail, whose book, *The End of Ice*, was published in 2019.[10] Jamail describes his discussions with leading scientists in the field, including those studying rising sea levels, weather disruption, the stress on forests and the consequences of the loss of glacial ice. In every case, Jamail says, the evidence is clear that a level of atmospheric warming unprecedented in human experience is already unavoidable, with consequences that are hard to imagine.

None of the three writers above is a scientist. That their conclusions, rather than those emanating from official reports from the scientific community, have seized some parts of the popular imagination may be due to genre. Neither the scientific method nor the way in which scientific understandings are expressed lend themselves readily to simple reading for the non-scientist. The scientific literature about climate change reflects the complexities of the world around us. It acknowledges, indeed, how little we know and how much we have yet to learn. The first part of Alastair Macintosh's book *Riders on the Storm*, though it pulls no punches about the gravity of the situation, is helpfully given over to an analysis of the position of the science in 2020, as it is reflected in the work of the IPCC (the Intergovernmental Panel on Climate Change).[11] Macintosh points out that due to the extraordinary rigour of the IPCC's methodology, the claims that it makes with 'high confidence' may not be based on the most up-to-date data and tend to be on the conservative or more cautious side. Nonetheless he believes that it is wise to base our own

---

[9] Jem Bendell, 'Deep Adaptation: A Map for Navigating Climate Tragedy' *IFLAS Occasional Paper 2, www.iflas.info*, revised version 2020 www.lifeworth.com/deepadaptation.pdf, accessed 24 October 2022.

[10] Dahr Jamail, *The End of Ice: Bearing Witness and Finding Meaning in the Path of Climate Disruption* (The New Press, 2020).

[11] Alastair McIntosh, *Riders on the Storm: The Climate Crisis and the Survival of Being* (Birlinn, 2020).

assessments on the IPCC's work, recognizing its comprehensiveness and thoroughness, while being aware that it is constantly under revision as new data comes to light. It is abundantly clear from what the scientists say that while extensive damage and loss is inevitable, human beings still have, in theory, the capacity to mitigate the worst effects of climate change, with its consequential degradation of the natural world and of human quality of life. The trouble is that we are so far from the position that we need to be in at the moment to do this. The result is a widespread sense of desperation and powerlessness, even of hopelessness.

Such hopelessness is an understandable emotional response in the current circumstances, a fact borne out by Bill McGuire in his book *Hothouse Earth*. McGuire *is* a scientist, and his work takes into account scientific observations up to 2021. Writing in 2022, in the light of the COP26 summit in Glasgow the previous autumn, he says:

> keeping this side of the 1.5C dangerous climate breakdown guardrail remains practically impossible ... the world continues to follow a path, based upon current policies and action, towards a hothouse future that would see a global average temperature rise of 2.7C by 2100 ... Be in no doubt, anything above 1.5C will see the advent of a world plagued by intense summer heat, extreme drought, devastating floods, reduced crop yields, rapidly melting ice sheets and surging sea levels. A rise of 2C and above will seriously threaten the stability of global society.[12]

---

[12] Bill McGuire, *Hothouse Earth: An Inhabitant's Guide* (Icon Books, 2022), 13.

3
AN EXISTENTIAL THREAT?
A QUESTION OF MEANING

Can climate change be described appropriately as an existential threat and, if so, what is meant by that term? The United Nations Secretary General has used the phrase, as have 'The Elders', the independent group of global leaders.[13] An existential threat is, obviously, at its worst, a threat to our biological life; to our continued existence. It signifies the possibility that the human species will disappear for ever, as is happening now to so many thousands of other species. Even if we do not accept that this is likely, climate change and its consequences can still pose a threat that we can legitimately call 'existential'.

Humanity has effected profound changes on the earth because it has evolved beyond an instinctive and non-reflective existence. Like bees and ants, we depend upon a social structure in which there are distinctive roles. To be human means that our sense of who we are is bound up with our social existence. Unlike the insects, though, we relate to one another as a matter of conscious choice, following patterns of behaviour and ways of seeing that we learn as we grow and develop.

Humans accordingly live by stories. From an early age our parents narrate or read them to us. In adulthood we continue to tell stories to ourselves and to each other: we read them in print

---

[13] www.un.org/sg/en/content/sg/statement/2018-09-10/secretary-generals-remarks-climate-change-delivered; theelders.org/news/five-reasons-climate-change-greatest-existential-threat-our-time, accessed 24 Oct 2022.

or hear them daily, some people write them or paint them or act them. By stories I mean accounts of events or aspects of experience or knowledge that follow a pattern or link things together. In this way they serve to make sense of the world we inhabit and of our individual and communal lives. Stories exist in many genres and perform a vast number of functions: persuading, educating, entertaining, giving comfort, providing security.

We exchange stories all the time, but we also live within them. A stable society relies on stories which broadly mean that its members are 'living in the same world'. In the high Middle Ages in Europe, the commonly-held story was the Christian one as it was then understood, as countless works of art demonstrate. With the advent of science during subsequent centuries in the rich and secure West, our confidence that we knew more thoroughly how the world worked grew, as the narrative became more secular. We assumed that, even with extreme events from time to time, our physical environment was relatively stable and consistent and could be relied upon to continue being so in the future. We felt comfortable in the cosmos. That assumption no longer holds. In the face of multiple global crises, many people have a sense that the old stories are no longer adequate to make sense of the present.

The sociologist Peter Berger illuminates why our situation poses such an existential threat.[14] Berger's work is built on the insight that the world in which we feel we live is, to a large extent, a human construction, a projection outwards of a shared set of assumptions about the nature of reality. To illustrate the role of imagination and belief in world-generation, we might consider a couple of childhood examples.

As a child I had an unquestioned and absolute belief in Father Christmas, as he was known in our house. Christmas for

[14] in Peter L. Berger and Thomas Luckmann, *The Social Construction of Reality: A Treatise in the Sociology of Knowledge* (Penguin, 1991).

me was a time of enchantment, which had little to do with the Christian narrative. I used to listen as hard as I could in the evening on Christmas Eve for the sound of the sleigh and the reindeer, always falling asleep before their arrival, but waking in the morning to find the full stocking at the foot of the bed. The disillusionment, when it came, was devastating. I can see now that I was projecting onto the world my conviction that Father Christmas was as real a person as my parents. Berger maintains that, as adults, we unwittingly collude in projecting onto the world our stories about what is real in the same, albeit more sophisticated, manner.

I also have a memory of a children's party when I was very young, at which there was a conjuror. One of the tricks he performed was the definitive one of the rabbit and the hat. The black top hat was shown to have nothing in it: it was placed upon the table, and covered with silks: magic words were murmured, and a live rabbit produced with a flourish from the previously empty hat. I recall the gasps of amazement from other children and from the adults present, which really puzzled me at the time. After all, a magician's role was to perform magic in the same way as the baker's role was to provide bread. What was so surprising about his producing a rabbit? Our understanding of, and beliefs about reality profoundly affect the way we experience things.

Peter Berger's work in *The Sacred Canopy* provides a persuasive analysis of the critical role of shared narratives in providing social stability. The nomos, the sense of order in which we live, is a human creation, a projection by us onto the cosmos. In turn—and this is a crucial concept for Berger—we humans then act as if our projections have an objective reality outside ourselves, and we allow ourselves to be constrained and directed by these external 'realities'. For social cohesion it is essential that the vast majority of people accept the prevailing nomos, a process that takes place largely unconsciously in childhood, as children absorb the tenets of the particular nomos in which they are raised. A moment's reflection indicates that our seven-day week, for instance, corresponds to no external, physical reality. Today is not objectively Saturday in any sense except that society has decided to agree on that. Yet Saturday does feel as though it has a kind of real, independent existence. I, for one, feel disorientated, a little unmoored, if I forget what day it is.

When the projection onto the cosmos incorporates ethical issues, and especially when a deity or deities of some kind are involved, then religion becomes an enormously powerful force. The god or gods that have been envisaged and projected out-wards are then—because their objective reality is assumed as part of the nomos—understood to require certain human re-sponses and behaviours. Right action is given divine sanction, and wrong actions can be portrayed as incurring the threat of divine retribution. This has strong political implications, to the extent that respecting the rule of law can be portrayed as obey-ing the will of God. When internalized by a majority, this assumption more-or-less guarantees social stability. The 'sacred canopy' of Berger's title alludes to the book of Isaiah:

> Then the LORD will create over the whole site of Mount Zion and over its places of assembly a cloud by day and smoke and the shining of a flaming fire by night. Indeed, over all the glory there will be a canopy. (Is. 4:5)

> On this mountain he will destroy the shroud that enfolds all peoples, the sheet that covers all nations. (Is. 25:7)

This refers to the way in which a shared belief in an om-nipotent and (when humoured) benign deity is a powerful shield for societies against the 'anomy', the lack of meaning and purpose, that would otherwise overwhelm them.

Berger goes out of his way to emphasize that in constructing his hypothesis he is doing so within an exclusively sociological frame. He was a committed Lutheran and well informed theologically. He is not making any judgement about the truth or otherwise of any particular nomos, about the extent to which our projections onto the cosmos are consonant with things as they actually are. What he does stress, though, is that the stability of society and the sense of selfhood of the individual is critically dependent on the acceptance of the nomos-myth, a myth which at the same time is dimly known to be a human construction. When that myth is threatened or collapses, both the social order and the sense of selfhood of the individual are at risk of being terminally undermined:

> It is thus possible to speak of collective as well as of individual states of anomy. In both cases, the fundamental order in terms of which the individual can 'make sense' of his life and recognize his own identity will be in process of disintegration. Not only will the individual then begin to lose his moral bearings, with disastrous psychological consequences, but he will become uncertain about his cognitive bearings as well. *The world begins to shake in the very instant that its sustaining conversation starts to falter.*[15]

This can indeed be described as an existential threat, a threat to our very existence, as we sense in the Anthropocene that the stories that define us are no longer tenable, that our sustaining conversations are faltering. Various responses are possible, and indeed are observable. A likely one is denial, which in this context means continuing to live by the old story while doing our best to suppress or argue away the unpleasant realities of any new one. Another is a strong sense of loss: loss of the old certainties, the old securities and, at its extreme, the loss of our identity. Fear and bewilderment can also feature, acknowledged

---

[15] Berger, *The Sacred Canopy*, 22 (my emphasis).

and expressed to varying degrees. When it comes to our faith, we may have a sense that the story we have lived by is no longer true and this can be devastating. We can feel that all our trust has been betrayed, that the God whose love and care we felt we knew has disappeared. We no longer know where we are with God. We may then stop believing and perhaps seek solace or diversion in ways that numb our anxieties without addressing them.

It is vital to acknowledge that faith is always rooted in assumptions about the nature of reality. If those assumptions are seen to be inadequate or false, then to leave behind our earlier concepts of God is an entirely rational response. Moreover, such a move is essential for the radical adaptation of our beliefs that the new situation requires. The difficulty of this should not be underestimated. In so far as religious faith serves to define our sense of who we are and where we place our trust, anything that is felt to be a serious threat to faith will shake us deeply. Even if we begin to accept that the old securities are no longer adequate, such a view may be rejected by others in our faith-community. Pastorally, it should be recognized that this can lead to a lonely place.

In 1961, Thomas Merton's spiritual journey had brought him into an 'engagement with the darkness of the world'. He experienced a 'growing feeling of alienation from his own monastic community, especially its "absurd optimism" and its attachment to the security of "right answers"'.[16] This resonates with some today who feel that the churches to which they belong have no shared understanding or expression about the extent of the climate crisis, continuing to assume a largely-unexamined optimism. At the least, such an attitude fails to recognize the plight of millions whose world is already ending as the changing climate destroys their way of life.

---

[16] Douglas E. Christie, *Blue Sapphire of the Mind: Notes for a Contemplative Ecology* (Oxford University Press, 2013), 307.

Merton was a contemplative, and exemplifies Peter Berger's claim that in every faith-tradition there are those who recognize that the 'institutional God' and, indeed, the God of our imagining are, to a considerable extent, human projections. The prophet is one who sees through the projections of the prevailing nomos and points to a deeper apprehension of reality. The apophatic tradition in its various forms in the world's faiths subverts the dangerous tendency to absolutize our inadequate and distorted claims about the nature and purposes of the Divine. The practice of the *via negativa* has important implications for the way in which we live in the uncertainties of the Anthropocene.

Acknowledging the threat to our sense of meaning is a first step towards recasting our narrative or, at the very least, finding different emphases within it. Given the magnitude of what is at stake globally in our present context, the strong possibility of unforeseen disasters and the intractable and long-term issues in play, it is likely that faith-communities and individual believers are also facing a sustained time of uncertainty and disagreement. In narrative terms these differences will be expressed in revised drafts of our story, in telling it from widely differing perspectives and, perhaps, in attempts to rewrite it altogether. Such a clamour of voices should not be silenced in the interest of trying to maintain the old certainties or in premature efforts to settle upon new ones. Rather, it should be welcomed as evidence of attempts to rewrite our story in a way that really works in the new context. This will be a messy and difficult business. Few would doubt that we are moving into a future that is more radically unpredictable and unknowable than has been the case for most of us in the past. It is a time when we must expect the unexpected, and our resilience will depend on our capacity to adapt to sudden and probably unwelcome changes in circumstance. This in turn will require that the narratives by which we make sense of things are held provisionally, and that we are open to questioning even the most fundamental of our beliefs.

That this is a vital pastoral concern as much as a theological one should be self-evident. Aimlessness, despair, violence and social chaos are the likely consequences of widespread loss of hope and sense of purpose. For that reason, those who adhere to the world's faiths have a responsibility not simply to react to events but to engage with them, to wrestle with the seemingly intractable realities of forces beyond our control, and to draw attention to the resources available to human beings beyond those of money and coercive power. This is inescapably a political task, for which the recasting of the stories that form us is vital and urgent work.

4
RECASTING OUR OWN STORIES

I had the great privilege of working in end-of-life care for nearly seven years. Subsequently I have come to realize that the impacts of our global climate and ecological crises have many parallels—on a different scale—to the trauma of a terminal diagnosis for an individual.

Good palliative care can, paradoxically, offer healing at the end of life. Where I worked, we offered people 'day hospice', giving them the opportunity, while they were still able to live at home, to spend a day with us once a week as their illness progressed. I am not a clinician, but I participated in many conversations with staff about what we were trying to do in that setting. As part of a health system driven by goals and outcomes, how might we define our activity? In one sense what we did had the worst possible outcome—the death of nearly every person we were caring for. A hospital in which ninety-nine percent of its patients died would soon be closed down. Nor were we especially in the business of prolonging life, which was the role of hospital-based oncologists and others. Gradually I came to recognize that much of our work was about the telling and, vitally, the recasting of stories.

To illustrate this, consider the following extract from a case presentation chosen more or less at random from a medical journal:

> A 75-year old female presented at the emergency room with dizziness, headache and vomiting for five days … She was referred

to the neurological service where a computerized tomography (CT) of the brain showed a left posterior fossa mass of high density, causing compression on the basal cistern and obstructive hydrocephalus ...[17]

This is a typical example of its type. Some of the language is highly technical and impenetrable for the non-specialist. By contrast, here is another statement:

It has almost been worth having terminal cancer, because hospice care has shown me for the first time what love really is.

Both of these quotations tell stories. They can be regarded as narratives that serve specific functions, and very different ones. The first is intentionally scientific, listing symptoms and observations in a concise and exact manner before, in a later part of the article, describing treatment and its outcome in terms of survival. This is the stuff of modern scientific medicine, the achievements of which in the reduction of pain and suffering, and the extension of our average lifespan have been extraordinary. The second short quotation, from one of our hospice patients, was reported to me by a colleague. The patient was a woman who had become terminally ill at a relatively early age, after a career that many would consider had been successful. At the day hospice, however, as the staff got to know her, she acknowledged that throughout her adult life her ambitions at work had been her only focus. Compelled by her illness to drop her frantic activity, she was at last able to get in touch with the parts of her personality that she had previously ruthlessly suppressed. This happened because she now understood what it meant to be accepted simply for who she was, and not for what

[17] S. F. Al-Dhahri, A. S. Al-Amro, W. Al-Shakwer, et al., 'Cerebellar Mass as a Primary Presentation of Papillary Thyroid Carcinoma: Case Report and Literature Review', *Head and Neck Oncology*, 1/23 (2009). https://doi.org/10.1186/1758-3284-1-23.

she could achieve. Rightly, she saw such acceptance as love, and it enabled her to face her dying much more peacefully and to enjoy more fully such living as remained to her.

Narratives are how we communicate meaning both to ourselves and to others about who we are and about our particular world. In our complex, multi-faceted lives we live with multiple narratives, some apparently self-contained, some obviously overlapping, some contradictory. For example, as a teenager I became acutely conscious that the person I was at school, the story that I inhabited with my friends there, was different from the story of who I was with my parents at home. That was why it was uncomfortable when the two worlds collided: when, for example, I was with my parents and met one of my school friends. Each separate story we live in and by, generates and gives shape to its own particular part of our world of meaning; together they contribute to, and perhaps even constitute, our individual identities. Of course, these stories differ greatly in their importance in our lives. Some cover and make sense of a limited aspect of our experience, whilst others have a greater scope and contribute much more fundamentally to who we are. Such 'wide scope' narratives—in Berger's terms what we might describe as our personal nomos—are vital for any feeling that the world is reasonably coherent and predictable, and they are therefore central to our security and wellbeing.

The extract from the journal article above is a typical example of what might be called the medical genre of narrative. Medicine has developed extremely efficient and specific techniques of recording and communicating information. Those who have been trained in it will know immediately, for instance, what the second part of the extract means. The rest of us, without a detailed knowledge of the precise vocabulary in play here, can gain at best only a vague idea that the patient's condition is a serious one.

The primary characteristics of this example of the medical genre of narrative are worth noting. The 'story' that is told is based almost entirely on observations of physical phenomena, most of them accurately measured or readily measurable with the right equipment. It is a list of facts, underpinned by a conceptual understanding of the way that physical, biological, and chemical processes interact in the human body. No emotions, either on the part of the patient or of the clinician, are recorded. This aspect of medical language is accurately echoed in the popular use of the adjective 'clinical' in the sense of coldness, of being without feeling. To say that is not to denigrate such language, which is highly effective in the environment for which it has been developed, nor is it to deny the deep sense of caring and vocation that clinicians bring to their work. It does, however, make the obvious but frequently under-appreciated point that in healthcare this way of telling the patient's story is strictly (and of necessity) limited in scope. The parallel with the scientific presentation of climate change is obvious. In official reports of their findings on climate change, scientists are required to suppress their own emotional responses and use their own clinical language, and that language may not speak to non-scientist readers with the impact or urgency that it should.

The words of the hospice patient tell a tale of an entirely different world of meaning. Although it is not the case that these words were spoken by the subject of the clinical description, it is illuminating to reflect that these words could have been about the same person. The patient's own words, few as they are, are an astonishing example of a 'wide scope' narrative. To start with, her brief 'story' covers the whole of her life up to that point, by implying that until then she had not understood what love really was. Secondly, as a statement about values and feelings, it refers to some of the most characteristic aspects of being human. Thirdly, it encompasses 'ultimacy', speaking of two of the things that are ultimately most important to us: love and death. In summary, it is a story about what is giving meaning to the speaker's current and difficult experience of life in a much richer way than the medical narrative can hope to do. That person, at that moment, was able to inhabit a profound story which was, to a large degree, *able to bear the burden of meaning of her illness.*

Many patients who came to the hospice felt defined by their diagnoses. With the extensive and often demanding range of treatments that they were often still undergoing, the constant reminders that they received from their symptoms or from the changed way their friends now related to them, it was easy for them to feel that they had shrunk just to 'someone dying of cancer'. In other words, the meaning in their lives was defined by the medical narrative in which they were living. It is easy in such circumstances for the whole horizon to be filled with awareness of, and worries about, illness. As we have seen, though, the medical narrative alone cannot bear the burden of the weight of meaning, cannot on its own bring happiness or peace or acceptance or reconciliation. That is why a huge part of the work of end-of-life care deliberately takes place outside the limits of the medical narrative. More accurately, it aims to provide a milieu of wide-scope narrative within which the medical narrative can take its rightful, crucial, but more-limited place. As Cicely Saunders (1918–2005), the founder of modern hospice practice, recognized and insisted, good medicine is absolutely vital to good palliative care, but it must always be in the service of living a life as fulfilled as possible within the constraints of the illness. Saunders never ceased emphasizing that care at the end of life must be holistic. She was driven by the conviction that healing, in its true sense of the restoration of wholeness, could take place even as someone was dying, and to this end she insisted on incorporating the clinical within a wider vision. Saunders's own wide-scope narrative was the Christian one, within which she developed her model of care.

A good part of the above can be read across to climate change. After severe trauma, a new identity in a changed world can be built. In palliative care the new identity is usually relatively short-lived, for obvious reasons. For us, who face the longer-term and unknown consequences of climate change, any rebuilding will be of a different character, assuming the world does have some kind of future, and that its illness is not in fact terminal. Certain aspects of the experience of living in our new world, though, are likely to be similar to the palliative care model. We will have a more radical uncertainty about the future. Like someone living with cancer, the underlying question will always be there: 'am I living or dying?' It can be hard to cope with the anxiety that is re-triggered by what could be suspicious symptoms, as it is with the extreme weather events that we experience or read about. End-of-life care is double-sided, as life in our new reality will have to be. The experience of palliative care shows how, in order to work towards acceptance at the end of life, the person who is terminally ill needs to reconcile two disparate narratives, the clinical, limited-scope one, and the wide-scope, values-based one. If the former can be held by and within the latter it is much more likely that some kind of meaning for the whole experience can be achieved, and peace of mind attained.

In the arena of responding to climate change the clinical narrative is the technological one. Whilst necessary and important, it is by no means the whole story; taking it as such indicates an over-mechanistic view of how the world works, a legacy of the seventeenth-century scientific revolution. The concentration of global attention to date almost exclusively on technological solutions to the climate crisis simply has not worked. Time and again we have heard that humanity has the tools to address the problem, if only it would act. The technological, clinical narrative, though, is simply unable of itself to generate the kind of response that is necessary to motivate action at the depth and scale needed. Such values as these can be found within the wide-scope narratives of faith, where wisdom has been accumulating for centuries. They can only be drawn out and put into practice, though, if the faiths can show that they now take into account fully the new external realities into which we are plunged. And, crucially, that they can express what they perceive in a new vision. 'Where there is no vision, the people perish' (Prov. 29:18 KJV) was the traditional way of putting this. The NRSV translates the same verse 'Where there is no prophecy, the people cast off restraint'. The parity of casting off restraint and perishing— death—between the translations is telling in our context. The existential crisis we face is caused by our lack of restraint in our use of the earth. However, what is needed first is vision, or prophecy, prophecy that inspires and promotes action.

Any new vision, new seeing, must make clear that we are all in exile from our pasts, our old environment, our old ways of living, our old ways of believing. Only if the vision or prophecy achieves this will faith carry conviction as a source of truth. As we sense that we are going into exile from the world as we knew it, previous understandings of our place in creation are being challenged. In Berger's terms, our old world is being deconstructed by external realities and the work of new world-construction has to begin urgently. To change the metaphor again, we are aware that the ship is sinking, and we have to build life-rafts as a matter of survival.

5
THE CREATED COSMOS

In the previous chapter I looked at what encountering our mortality can teach us about confronting climate change, and the importance of our narratives for our wellbeing. The parallels are not exact though: for one thing, it is the whole earth that is dying, or which at least has a life-limiting illness. In our present situation we humans are both the patient facing death and the family facing bereavement. In other ways climate change is much more threatening than our routine mortality. We have been living with the knowledge of individual death for millennia, but always against a background of relative stability in the environment that sustains us. There has usually been a reasonable expectation that a bad harvest will be followed by a better one, that rain will end drought before total desolation. People at the end of life have gained hope from a predictable future, that they will leave behind a legacy that will live on after them in their works or their offspring, something that cannot now be assured. My death, and those of others, have been seen as paragraphs in an ongoing story that is assumed to have a consistent underlying plot from the past, through the present, and into the future. Individual trauma and loss of meaning has usually taken place against the background of a stable context to which the traumatized have to reorientate themselves, to relate in a new way to a normality that is taken for granted. But normality, in the sense of stability and predictability, is fast disappearing.

Climate change threatens us with a turning of the page after which we find ourselves in an entirely different story, one in which we have no clue about the plot. If even the middle of the range of possible futures is realized, the world that is coming upon us may well be so different from our present one as to be beyond our current ability to imagine it. This is a fundamental difficulty in pastoral approaches to the unprecedented threat of climate change. Prior experience can provide no assured analogies to help us envisage future circumstances. No wonder this feels like an existential threat.

I argued above that the development of individual and social resilience for a threatening future, while we begin to shape new stories fit for a new age, will depend on our holding our narratives provisionally. This is not something we have been used to. For some believers especially, 'articles of faith' have been seen as non-negotiable and unchanging. But if we are to find our way forward with integrity, we must accept that many of our prior assumptions are no longer true. If we are honest, we are faced with novel and acute questions about our place in the world, and the meaning—if any—of humanity's place in the cosmos. These questions become evident once we grasp the implications of two relatively recent areas of scientific discovery, namely the extent of the universe and the workings of the ecosphere.

The Christian picture of time and history, in the form that many have received and currently envisage it, is inadequate for the Anthropocene. It could plausibly be assumed until the end of the eighteenth century that the universe had remained largely unchanged since God had made it, that the purposes of God for the whole of creation were to be worked out on behalf of human beings, and that the 'cosmic Christ' would return at the end of time to initiate a new heaven and a new earth. Cosmology (in the sense of the understanding of the physical universe) and theology, although showing strains in their relationship, were still able to retain aspects of the synthesis that had characterized the medieval period. The reality of climate change compels us to face up to the gradual severing, over the last 250 years or so, of the points of contact between the old Christian account of the purposes of God in history on the one hand, and our conception of the physical universe on the other.

The parting of the ways has been a strategic retreat, perhaps seen as a judicious withdrawal from some outlying territory in order to safeguard the centre. I suspect that for most Christians, at least in the West, the question of how the physical world works has been entirely surrendered to science. Pierre-Simon Laplace allegedly said that 'I have no need of that hypothesis' when asked by Napoleon where God fitted into his theory on the origin of the solar system. Certainly, it does seem to be the case that science so far has managed to explain the world without reference to the metaphysical. Potentially that still leaves a wide field for faith in the areas of beauty and mystery, expressed through poetry and metaphor as that which points to a different kind of truth and meaning. However, to see factual truth and poetic truth in a dualistic way, as inhabiting separate, unrelated worlds of meaning, is an error that becomes apparent in the face of real-world trauma. In such circumstances harsh questions about the truth of our faith and in what we really put our trust become urgent, just as they may do for the person with a terminal illness.

The unavoidable realities of climate change certainly bring into sharper focus what can be felt as an uneasy tension between two competing narratives. On the one hand faith says that God is in all things and all things are in God: time's arrow points in the direction of the return of all things to God through Christ. On the other hand, the scientific account of the physical world says that human life may well destroy itself just as it has already destroyed uncountable numbers of species in recent times; that humanity might have no long-term future in the universe. Is it still possible to order our narratives so that the wide-scope story of God can encompass and hold the scientific account of the world? If it is not, then Christian faith shrinks to a comforting fantasy.

In 1952 J. B. Phillips published his book with the self-explanatory title *Your God is Too Small*.[18] Now, even more than then, we need to ask ourselves whether our concepts of God are adequate given the scale and complexities of the universe that science has revealed to us in recent decades. We speak sometimes rather glibly of God in creation, and creation in God: and then we read that 'Astronomers estimate there could be anywhere from 300-million to 40-billion Earth-like planets in the Milky Way', that 'Even if just a fraction of those planets developed the conditions necessary for the existence of life, there would still be millions of planets in our galaxy alone that are home to living things.'[19] While estimates among different experts vary, an acceptable range of the number of galaxies is between 100 billion and 200 billion, most of which contain a hundred billion stars or more.[20]

Is our God too small? Or does a universe on this scale make our God simply inconceivable? If this recognizes with the psalmist that 'Such knowledge is too wonderful for me' (Ps. 139:6), it should also help us to see again how infinitely smaller we humans are in the scale of things than the ancient writers understood. As evolved and evolving animals we are fleetingly transient in the great scheme of things. This is important as we face the real possibility of human extinction. It may indeed be

---

[18] J. B. Phillips, *Your God is Too Small: A Guide for Believers and Skeptics Alike* (Epworth Press, 1952).

[19] Based on data from the Kepler and other planet-hunting telescopes. www.worldatlas.com/space/how-many-earth-like-planets-are-there-in-the-milky-way.html, accessed 20 April 2023.

[20] www.space.com/25303-how-many-galaxies-are-in-the-universe.html, accessed 20 April 2023.

that God's 'human experiment' will fail here on this planet. To see this is also to face the collapse of our faith-nomos, of our over-arching narrative about an omnipotent, omniscient God who, in His wisdom, chose human beings uniquely as the way of bringing the whole cosmos back to God. Whilst faith may continue to hope that this may be so, it will surely not be so in any way that we used to imagine it. The universe that Bishop Ussher, Isaac Newton and Johannes Kepler inhabited less than four centuries ago was miniscule both in space and time compared to ours, and was believed to be no more than around 6,000 years old. The end of all things, which Jesus described, when 'the sun will be darkened, and the moon will not give its light, and the stars will be falling from heaven, and the powers of the heavens will be shaken' (Mark 13:24) could then be readily understood as a literal description of events. Now, we see that if the physical forces in the universe continue to operate as they appear to have done since the 'Big Bang', then even our own sun has about five billion years to shine before it darkens.

We can learn from the past about the need to reconcile the observed universe and our structures of meaning. Although it is almost impossible to enter into the world view of previous eras, to experience the world as it was experienced then, the writings that have come down to us show that the separation of physics and metaphysics would probably have been incomprehensible in most pre-scientific societies.

This was the case for ancient Israel, as is clear from the Tanakh. Painstaking scholarship in recent decades has shed fascinating light on this ancient entwining of metaphysics, cultic practice, and the world as it was observed. The Qumran discoveries have revealed how the Essenes around the time of Jesus passionately adhered to a 364-day calendar. Because such a calendar enables a year to be divided into four equal quarters and exactly fifty-two weeks of seven days it reflects the original perfection of creation. This perfection was marred first by the rebellious angels among whose ranks are now 'wandering stars' (the planets, the sun and the moon) who refuse to keep their intended place in the Divine order. Therefore, those who follow a calendar that is synchronous with the observed solar year are apostates in the view of the Essenes, and their ritual practices will fall on the 'wrong' days, a matter of supreme moment for the Temple cult. The members of the Qumran community believed that they followed the true, Divine seasons, and that it was the observed seasons that were out of synchronicity with God's intention at creation and throughout time.[21]

The Qumran community's beliefs illuminate clearly how assumptions about cosmology influence religious belief and practice. The Essenes had projected onto the universe a systematic and coherent structure of meaning—a 'cosmotheology'— that was ultimately doomed because it fell far short of physical and therefore theological truth. The Essenes' accepted narrative was objectively and, from our perspective, obviously fragile, but then so is every narrative, *including ours*. It is worth bearing in mind the extraordinary tenacity of well-established narratives. A good example is the Ptolemaic model of the universe, formulated in the second century AD. It assumed a stationary earth at the centre with the sun, moon, and all the planets in circular orbits. The latter assumption derived from the Greek idea of perfection in the heavens. Subsequent observations showed that Ptolemy's original model did not explain the way that planets actually moved, but instead of questioning the basic model, awkward adjustments were added to account for the discrepancies. It took sixteen centuries before the German astronomer and mathematician Johannes Kepler (1571–1630) demonstrated

---

[21] For more on the Essenes, see Alfred Osborne, *A Cosmic Liturgy: Qumran's 364-Day Calendar* (Brepols, 2019). For the links between the Jewish Temple and the ancient covenant of creation, see Margaret Barker, *Temple Theology: An Introduction* (SPCK, 2004), chapter 2.

that the concept of circular orbits was incompatible with the way the planets moved in space.

Where are the Essenes now? Their faith-community did not survive in the long term because the cosmos in which they believed and the God they projected was out of kilter with what, from our current perspective, we call 'reality'. We can see that they were living under the domination of a false narrative, one that was too narrow in scope. Peter Berger's work sheds light for us on how important a communally-held cosmology is for social stability, and at the same time why an embedded cosmology is so hard to give up. Accepting such change may be seen as threatening to the social order and, most importantly, as threatening the sense of selfhood of the individual. Failure to accept reality against irrefutable evidence, though, is a road leading towards tragedy. We do not need to look as far back as the Essenes or Ptolemy to see how tenacious a false cosmotheology can be: a substantial number of US citizens, for example, continue to believe in the literal truth of the creation stories in Genesis.[22]

---

[22] The number appears to be decreasing and poll data can be misleading. See for instance the article by Cary Funk, Greg Smith and David Masci in *Scientific American*, 12 February 2019: blogs.scientificamerican.com/observations/how-many-creationists-are-there-in-america/, accessed 10 May 2023, in which the proportion varied from 18% to 31% depending on how the question was couched.

6
CREATION AND COVENANT

The example of the Essenes shows the futility of clinging to a particular cosmology or theology when the evidence against it becomes overwhelming. How should we revise our own inherited cosmological and theological assumptions about humanity's place in the Divine scheme of things when they are undermined by emerging evidence about how the world works? One approach is to consider the understanding of 'covenant'. The concept of covenant is fundamental to Jewish faith. It is much more than a contract, a binding agreement between two parties. In the Tanakh it defined the special identity of the Jewish people as being uniquely chosen to receive and follow God's laws, and thereby to fulfil their central role in the divine plan for the whole of creation.

The Tanakh illustrates how the perspective on covenant changed and developed over time. Some implications of the early understanding of the covenant are disturbing, if not shocking, today. In our terms, the promise to Abraham that his descendants would receive the land of Canaan as a perpetual possession was used to justify wholesale slaughter. 'So Joshua defeated the whole land … he … utterly destroyed all that breathed, as the Lord God of Israel commanded' (Josh. 10:40). We would call this genocide. It does not matter how true the stories are, or the real historical extent of the casualties, what is significant is that the writers and redactors of these accounts considered such massacres as illustrative of the divine will, acting on their special behalf.

This early understanding had a self-absorbed focus, and although the individual 'alien' was to be afforded respect and certain rights, the place of non-Jews in God's plan was ambiguous:

> You shall not deprive a resident alien or an orphan of justice; you shall not take a widow's garment in pledge. Remember that you were a slave in Egypt and the Lord your God redeemed you from there; therefore I command you to do this. (Deut. 24:17)

> When you beat your olive trees, do not strip what is left; it shall be for the alien, the orphan, and the widow. When you gather the grapes of your vineyard, do not glean what is left; it shall be for the alien, the orphan, and the widow. (Deut. 24:20–1)

This perspective had to be widened after the disasters of the destruction of the Jerusalem Temple in 586 BC, the subsequent forced exile to Babylon, and again after the Roman sacking of both the second Temple and the city in AD 70. These crises forced a broader understanding of covenant. God no longer just dwelt in the 'promised land', and no longer could the Jerusalem Temple be the primary locus of God's encounter with God's people. With the Jewish people dispersed, they began to realize that they were covenanted not just in their own interests but in those of all the nations, to whom they should demonstrate how to live and organize their societies in fulfilment of God's plan:

> And the foreigners who join themselves to the Lord,
> to minister to him, to love the name of the Lord,
> and to be his servants,
> all who keep the sabbath, and do not profane it,
> and hold fast my covenant—
> these I will bring to my holy mountain,
> and make them joyful in my house of prayer;
> their burnt offerings and their sacrifices
> will be accepted on my altar;
> for my house shall be called a house of prayer
> for all peoples. (Is. 56:6–7)

This extension of the notion of God's covenant primarily being with one small people was also developed in the early Christian church. The contentious early-Christian debates, of which we have glimpses in the Messianic Writings, resulted in the claim that all people everywhere were potentially within the covenant, all equally loved as they followed Jesus, no matter what their background or origin.

St Paul's bold, revolutionary and highly political statement that 'There is no longer Jew or Greek, there is no longer slave or free, there is no longer male and female; for all of you are one in Christ Jesus.' (Gal. 3:28) is still challenging today. Paul's enlarged vision of covenant needs now, well before its full realization in our social and political lives, to be supplanted by one that is still wider. Each broadening of the scope of covenant—in every case prompted by extreme experience of one kind or another—tends to modify or reduce the centrality in the Divine Plan of the self-perceived 'special group', or those we define as 'us' as opposed to 'them'. The small tribal people of early Judaism came gradually to see that 'their' God also cared for the other nations. The little Jewish sect following the risen Messiah Jesus realized that the Gentiles were now included within the 'us'. The urgent step for the Christian understanding of covenant is to accept that the doctrine of the central role in the whole cosmos afforded by God to human beings is no longer tenable in the way that it was. We are not as special as we thought we were, or, better, the rest of creation is, in its own way, as special as us.

According to the Genesis narrative, there was an earlier covenant than that with Abraham. This was the covenant that God revealed after the Great Flood had destroyed every living creature except those who had been kept safe in the ark:

> Then God said to Noah and to his sons with him, "As for me, I am establishing my covenant with you and your descendants after you, and with every living creature that is with you, the

birds, the domestic animals, and every animal of the earth with you, as many as came out of the ark. I establish my covenant with you, that never again shall all flesh be cut off by the waters of a flood, and never again shall there be a flood to destroy the earth." (Gen. 9:8–11)

God is described in the above passage as speaking both to Noah *and* to his sons. More usually in the tradition, the covenant or its implications are revealed to chosen individuals: Abraham, Moses, Isaiah, Ezekiel, and so on. The new post-Diluvian covenant is revealed to the whole family (sidestepping the modern question of whether Mrs Noah and her daughters-in-law were included in the revelation). It is a covenant which, uniquely in the biblical canon, also applies universally and equally to human and other forms of life. Every living creature, in this sense, has equal value. The Flood narrative constitutes a second act of creation that moderates the primacy of the human portrayed in Genesis 1:

God blessed them, and God said to them, 'Be fruitful and multiply, and fill the earth and subdue it; and have dominion over the fish of the sea and over the birds of the air and over every living thing that moves upon the earth.' (Gen. 1:28)

Taking creation seriously must mean, for Christians, a great deal more than trying to live sustainably on a finite planet, though of course it does mean that too. It especially requires those of us who have inherited the Western post-Reformation tradition to recognize how limited and damaging a strong and self-centred focus on individual salvation has been. Such reflections should prompt us to redefine (by enlarging its scope) the 'everlasting covenant' spoken of in Isaiah 24:

The earth lies polluted
    under its inhabitants;
for they have transgressed laws,
    violated the statutes,
    broken the everlasting covenant. (Is. 24:5)

If we wish to talk meaningfully of 'God's creation' then that must refer to the whole universe in all its unimaginable size. Yes, human beings are included in the covenant relationship in their own unique way, but an up-to-date 'cosmotheology' must place a significant question mark over any claim that human uniqueness is accompanied by uniquely-special privileges throughout the universe. The case has been argued that our universe had to be the way it is if God wished to bring into being a self-aware, rational creature with genuine agency; a theological take on the anthropic principle. It is a further step, though, to extend that concept to claim that humanity is indispensable to the Divine Plan for the entire cosmos. We just do not know what other forms of life and consciousness may exist elsewhere in the universe, and we have no grounds for ruling out *a priori* the possibility that God may have revealed God's self to them also, within their own idiom.

7
HUMAN BEINGS IN THE WORLD

A widening of the scope of covenant can help in the re-ordering of our faith-narrative to take account of the unimaginable scale of the universe. This, though, comes at the cost of surrendering the assumptions of earlier eras about the unique and central role of human beings in the cosmos. Prior beliefs about humanity's proper place only on the planet are also undermined by recent science. Here is another area in which, both for our future and for our mental wellbeing, we need to realign our stories with the way the natural world—our 'environment'—actually works.

Whatever their professed doctrinal beliefs, there is little doubt that most Western Christians, in common with their secular counterparts, have tended to follow mainstream assumptions about the working of the non-human world, while simultaneously acting in ways that ignore current science. Lynn White's famous 1967 essay laid the responsibility for our current utilitarian approach to the natural world squarely at the door of Christianity.[23] Whatever one thinks of White's argument, he drew attention very acutely to the way we tend to perceive ourselves: 'Despite Copernicus, all the cosmos rotates around our little globe. Despite Darwin, we are not, in our hearts, part of the natural process.'[24] Most of us seem, indeed, to go about our daily

---

[23] Lynn White, Jr, 'The Historic Roots of our Ecologic Crisis', *Science*, New Series, 155/3767 (March 1967), 1203–7, available on the website of the *Interdisciplinary Encyclopedia of Religion and Science*, ed. by G. Tanzella-Nitti, I. Colagè and A. Strumia: www.inters.org/files/white1967.pdf, accessed 10 May 2023.

[24] White, 'The Historic Roots of our Ecologic Crisis', 1206, col. 3.

business with precisely that outlook, one in which the world is experienced as radiating out from us and is subject to our manipulation and control. As White rather brutally put it at a time when human threats to the environment on a global scale were only beginning to be acknowledged:

> To a Christian a tree can be no more than a physical fact. The whole concept of the sacred grove is alien to Christianity and to the ethos of the West ... Hence we shall continue to have a worsening ecologic crisis until we reject the Christian axiom that nature has no reason for existence save to serve man.[25]

White referred to Christianity as 'the most anthropocentric religion the world has seen', but the assumption that human beings are uniquely different from the rest of creation has gradually and extensively been qualified by revelations from every branch of the natural sciences. The modern western erosion of the idea of human exceptionalism perhaps began with Darwin, and there seems to be an accelerating trend of discoveries accelerating the process. To affirm, for example, that humans are animals is not to deny the extraordinary abilities of our species; but neither must we ignore the extraordinary abilities of other species. Human senses only have access to a limited spectrum of information, and therefore the world we construct from our sense-data is not the world as it is, but only one way of experiencing and living in it. Other creatures that share the planet with us live in a multiplicity of different worlds that we can no more experience than they can experience ours. As Karl Barth (rather surprisingly) wrote: 'We do not really know that the outer circle of all other creatures exists for the inner circle of humanity. The very opposite may well be the case.'[26]

---

[25] Ibid.

[26] Karl Barth, *Church Dogmatics*, III/2,138, quoted by Timothy Gorringe, in *Word, Silence, and the Climate Emergency: God, Ekklesia, and Christian Doctrine* (Lexington Books/Fortress Academic, 2020), 306.

This concept goes even deeper: it is becoming ever more apparent that humans are as embedded in, as entwined with, their environment as are all other beings. Only recently have we begun to comprehend, or to re-learn, that in the physical world a wood does not just consist of separate entities happening to coexist within certain boundaries. On the contrary, each entity only has its being through its dynamic, constantly changing relationships with the rest of the system upon which it depends and which it influences in turn. Merlin Sheldrake's fascinating account of the extraordinary world of fungi, *Entangled Life*, explores this recently discovered reality powerfully and at times disturbingly.[27]

Such an altered perspective has important implications for the Christian understanding of creation. We humans can only exist as integral parts of the whole ecosphere: we are embedded in it and fundamentally dependent upon it. Therefore we must see creation holistically. We still talk about 'us' as separate from 'the environment', as though we are indeed the *deus ex machina*. But we are not: it is worth bearing in mind that for all other creatures human beings are an aspect of, and an invasion into, their environment. From the point of view of creation absolutely everything is 'the environment'.

The old idea of a world created by God for human beings to live in, whereby the non-human only has its value in so far as it promotes human wellbeing, is dangerously out of date. To the Christian in the Anthropocene, a tree must be much more than a physical fact. Either the 'whole system' has ultimate value, or none of it has. This whole system involves a continuous flow and exchange between all things; bringing into existence new manifestations of life and the passing of older ones, always bound together inextricably by interdependence.

---

[27] Merlin Sheldrake, *Entangled Life: How Fungi Make our Worlds, Change our Minds and Shape our Futures* (The Bodley Head, 2020).

Creation seen in this way encourages us to reaffirm the sacred aspect of the grove.

We now understand that we live in an evolving universe, and that ongoing evolution is intrinsic to what we call creation. Darwin showed how competition within and between species was a key aspect of evolution, indicating an inescapable harshness and relentlessness in the process. Nonetheless nature, red in tooth and claw, is far from an adequate summary of how the living world works: Colin Tudge in *The Great Re-Think* makes clear that cooperation and mutualism seems to be the deeper truth.[28] However, science shows clearly that any ecosphere can only operate within defined and relatively narrow limits. Once these limits are pushed the whole system shows signs of stress, and if they are exceeded then wide-scale collapse can result. In the past, volcanic activity, changes in atmospheric and oceanic chemistry, and other natural occurrences over a geologically brief timescale were triggers for mass extinctions. Over the millennia, species that emerged and flourished have become extinct when their environment altered at a rate exceeding their capacity to adapt.[29]

We are now in the situation where human activity is triggering another mass extinction, the implications of which cannot be predicted. The ecosphere as we know it, which has enabled and nurtured human life, may collapse. Some inhabited areas of the globe are already becoming unliveable for humans because of rising temperatures, a trend that will almost certainly accelerate. We are rapidly altering our own environment beyond our capacity to adapt.

---

[28] Colin Tudge, *The Great Re-Think: A 21st Century Renaissance* (Pari Publishing, 2020), 91ff.

[29] University of California at Berkeley Museum of Paleontology 'Understanding Evolution' online teaching resources on evolution and extinction drawing on current research: evolution.berkeley.edu/mass-extinction/what-causes-mass-extinctions/, accessed 8 May 2023.

In purely physical terms we are at grave risk of degrading our environment to such an extent that it can no longer sustain human life. The crucial difference, though, between the previous mass extinctions and the present one—which may include us— is that this one has been brought about by our own choices to ignore not just the physical but also the ethical dimensions of the world's deep structure. Ethically, as well as physically, our species is currently 'not fit to survive'. The kind of fitness that we need is, ironically, the exact opposite of that which is promoted by social Darwinism.

8
ETHICS AND ECOSPHERE

Specifically Christian creation ethics should perhaps begin, not from Genesis 1:26,

> Then God said, 'Let us make humankind in our image, according to our likeness; and let them have dominion over the fish of the sea, and over the birds of the air, and over the cattle, and over all the wild animals of the earth, and over every creeping thing that creeps upon the earth.'

nor from the covenant with Noah and his family, but from the prologue of John's Gospel. This is, after all, yet another creation story in addition to the ones we find in the Tanakh. The placing of two creation stories at the beginning of our Testaments tends to set up a particular perspective on God's relationship to creation. The picture as it was painted for me in childhood was of God making the physical world, revealing God's nature and requirements, first to the Jewish nation, then coming to earth in the person of Jesus to fulfil the plan of salvation. The created order was implicitly presented as a form of static stage-set where humans lived out their lives on the way towards their ultimate and eternal destiny beyond this world. That kind of background assumption, if established at an early age, can continue to linger persistently and subtly influence our reading of the Scriptures. As we saw above, though, the world is not a static stage-set on which we strut and fret: we are both players and scenery in a complex network of dynamic and constantly changing interaction.

John's assertion is that the truest glimpse we can obtain of God's 'character' is in Jesus:

> Jesus said to him, "Have I been with you all this time, Philip, and you still do not know me? Whoever has seen me has seen the Father. How can you say, 'Show us the Father'?" (John 14:9)

If Jesus as the Word was also the one through whom the world was made, then it seems difficult to reduce physical creation merely to morally neutral 'stuff'. There is no place here for any separation of the sacred and the profane: nothing is outside the Temple because Jesus is the New Temple. John's Logos refers to Wisdom as portrayed in the Wisdom tradition and perhaps especially the creation story of Proverbs 8:

> The Lord created me at the beginning of his work,
> the first of his acts of long ago.
> Ages ago I was set up,
> at the first, before the beginning of the earth.
> When there were no depths I was brought forth,
> when there were no springs abounding with water.
> Before the mountains had been shaped,
> before the hills, I was brought forth —
> when he had not yet made earth and fields,
> or the world's first bits of soil.
> When he established the heavens, I was there,
> when he drew a circle on the face of the deep,
> when he made firm the skies above,
> when he established the fountains of the deep,
> when he assigned to the sea its limit,
> so that the waters might not transgress his command,
> when he marked out the foundations of the earth,
> then I was beside him, like a master worker;
> and I was daily his delight,
> rejoicing before him always,
> rejoicing in his inhabited world
> and delighting in the human race. (Prov. 8:22–31)

Wisdom here—feminine in Hebrew grammar—is deeply involved in creation not simply as an organizing principle (the rational dimension, the *logos* of Greek philosophy) but also as personhood (the ethical, 'passionate' dimension). John is saying that Jesus revealed, through his life, death and resurrection, the underlying and inherent nature of the entire created order—'all that was made'. That order has the same 'character' as the one we discern in the incarnate Jesus. In order to know how to live in harmony with the rest of creation, we should start with Jesus as the revelation of God's nature. From that understanding we can work towards a truthful way of living within the animate and inanimate world around us.

Humankind has always recognized that it is surrounded by powerful and invisible forces over which it seems to have little control. In ancient times dramatic and unusual weather events, earthquakes and other natural disasters were often interpreted as the direct actions of God or the gods. Such events, therefore, were imbued with ethical significance, and could be a warning or a punishment. Now we explain such things in the impersonal terms of physics or geology, with the result that the majority of people in the West see no ethical significance whatsoever in the so-called 'laws of nature'. For instance, instead of frequent floods being understood as a consequence of immorality or an unjust social system, they are merely a technical problem to be solved through gaining control over the invisible forces that determine atmospherics and hydraulics. If we follow the scriptural insights, this is an error, and a profound one. Of course, it is good to move beyond naive superstition, and to acknowledge that indeed the rain falls on the just and the unjust alike (Matt. 5:45); but there is a difference between that and the recognition, perceived as preposterous by many, that our climate and biodiversity crises are the result of unethical behaviour that is fundamentally antithetical to reality.

If the Word from God determines the deep structure and direction of the cosmos, then we are mistaken when we regard the invisible natural forces as impersonal and, in principle, open to being directed in whatever way we choose without adverse consequences. On the contrary: not only do these forces reflect the Divine character in some profound way, which always works in a life-enhancing direction, but we interfere with those forces casually at our peril. Such a shift in perspective radically alters any Christian approach to 'the environment'. Humanity's vocation, more than ever in this time of imminent disaster, should now be seen as requiring us to discern and to work in harmony with the deep structure of reality, with the crucial recognition that this is an ethical and not just a technological imperative. We have a responsibility to creation rather than for it. Our basic orientation should be towards the good of others, rather than that of ourselves, as the Christian Gospel and many other traditions have always maintained. Now, though, we need to see ourselves as also being in service to the worlds of the oak tree and the gannet, of the elephant and the primrose, on their own terms. The interests of the honeybee and of the rainforest are both to be respected as contributing to the interests of the whole, and as having intrinsic value quite independent of the human perspective on them.

From this altered viewpoint we can see more clearly how the covenant is with the whole community of creation, which means that every part of it must be taken seriously as a reflection of the ongoing creative activity of the Logos. The gulf between the implications of this realization for our economic and social order and current practice could, even now, hardly seem wider. There are daily reports indicating that, although some progress is being made in the right direction, that progress is being comprehensively overridden by the juggernaut of consumerism and materialism. To take one example out of hundreds, nineteen scientists published an article in January

2021 with the self-explanatory title 'Underestimating the Challenges of Avoiding a Ghastly Future'.[30] It is salutary to set this alongside just one random example: the use of polyester in clothing has doubled globally in 20 years and continues to increase, with huge implications for microplastic pollution and the continued use of fossil fuels.[31] In the planetary context the warning of Isaiah no longer seems like outdated superstition:

> The earth dries up and withers,
>> the world languishes and withers;
>> the heavens languish together with the earth.
> The earth lies polluted
>> under its inhabitants; for they
> have transgressed laws,
>> violated the statutes,
>> broken the everlasting covenant.
> Therefore a curse devours the earth,
>> and its inhabitants suffer for their guilt. (Is. 24:4–6)

It is vital to recognize that, while covenant promises are unbreakable from God's side, this does not give human beings licence to ignore them yet still expect them to be fulfilled. Every covenant promise is conditional for its realization on the faithful response of those with whom it is made. Although—as in the Noahic covenant of Genesis 9—this requirement may not be explicitly stated, nonetheless the whole witness of the Tanakh shows it to be the case, as for example in the Isaiah passage above. See also, for instance, Jeremiah chapters 11–15, where drought and destruction in Israel and Judah is again portrayed as the result of failure to obey the word of the Lord:

---

[30] Corey J. A. Bradshaw et al., 'Underestimating the Challenges of Avoiding a Ghastly Future', *Frontiers in Conservation Science*, 1/615419 (Jan 2021), available at: www.frontiersin.org/articles/10.3389/fcosc.2020.615419/full, accessed 20 April 2023.

[31] https://www.edie.net/fast-fashion-polyester-production-has-doubled-since-2000-with-huge-climate-implications/.

For I solemnly warned your ancestors when I brought them up out of the land of Egypt, warning them persistently, even to this day, saying, Obey my voice. Yet they did not obey or incline their ear, but everyone walked in the stubbornness of an evil will. So I brought upon them all the words of this covenant, which I commanded them to do, but they did not. … Therefore, thus says the LORD, assuredly I am going to bring disaster upon them that they cannot escape; though they cry out to me, I will not listen to them. (Jer. 11:7–8, 11)

We can now see that such divine 'punishments' are not the vengeful acts of a jealous God. They are an inevitable consequence of human societies choosing to act against the grain of the created order, the nature of which is revealed in the creating, sustaining and incarnate Logos. A Logos which, paradoxically, is not one of domination and control, but rather of compassion, tenderness, and a yearning for justice that yet will not break the bruised reed (Is. 42:3).

Somehow we have to hold in balance, perhaps in creative tension, our commitment to a God of *hesed*, of steadfast love and compassion, with the God of the Greek *logos*, of rational order. Both of these are equally aspects of the Word—the Word of Wisdom, rather than the word of Greek philosophy. The Logos dimension is essential if we are to exist in a reasonably predictable universe, one in which the 'laws of physics' operate reliably. Particle physics has shown us how such order actually arises out of radical unpredictability, which subverts the closed determinism implied by the Newtonian clockwork universe. It also reminds us of the folly of holding hubristic notions of complete understanding and control of natural phenomena (which is a tendency much more in political thinking than in science). Word, Logos, Spirit, God, Love and so on are names we give to our fragmentary glimpses of the mystery of the Ultimate in creation and creation in the Ultimate.

The old religious instincts that linked right ethical behaviour to the flourishing of the land, and vice versa were, in essence, correct, although their explanations of the way in which this happened were inadequate. The God of the Tanakh was very hands-on at times, even able to make the sun and moon stand still (Josh. 10:12), the sun move backwards (Is. 38:8), to bring storms (Jer. 10:13), and in numerous other ways to direct natural phenomena in an immediate way. However, the way in which ethical behaviour affects the weather is more subtle. It is not via the immediate intervention of God but through the degree to which human society aligns with the Logos, the Logos of God the creator which/who has both ethical character and direction. This is indeed the 'everlasting covenant' of Isaiah and brings the climate crisis right back into the centre of personal morality, and of economics, politics and justice at the social level. The Ten Words spoken to Israel at Mount Sinai are the prototype of the basic requirements not just of a healthy society but of a healthy earth as well, without which a healthy society cannot be sustained. This is why climate justice is arguably even more fundamental to a sustainable future than the reliance on technology that is so often seen as the sole answer to ecological damage.

The most cursory survey of the state of the world in the first quarter of the twenty-first century indicates that we are in deep trouble. We see how the political and economic systems of the most powerful countries are mainly structured to work in the opposite direction to that of the Logos and, moreover, to make a perverse virtue of that. It is hardly surprising that many people are in despair and see no hope.

9
REPENTANCE, LAMENT AND GRIEF

The former Astronomer Royal, Sir Martin Rees, said in 2004 that in his view the human race had only a fifty-fifty chance of surviving the present century. Since then, if the science is to be believed, the odds against humanity have worsened considerably. Deep-rooted anxiety about the ecological situation is not only widespread but also an entirely rational response.

Honest recognition of the fact of irreversible, profound loss, is about being open to suffering when it is unavoidable. Such acceptance is almost always accompanied by deep grief, a grief that nonetheless has the possibility to be the soil which nurtures hope. In 587 BC King Nebuchadnezzar of Babylon captured and destroyed the city of Jerusalem, subsequently deporting many of the prominent citizens of Judah to Babylon. The Prophet Jeremiah was a witness to these traumatic events and in two books, Jeremiah and Lamentations, gives both descriptive and poetic voice to his experience. The vision is often one of utter desolation:

> I looked on the earth, and lo, it was waste and void;
>> and to the heavens, and they had no light.
> I looked on the mountains, and lo, they were quaking,
>> and all the hills moved to and fro.
> I looked, and lo, there was no one at all,
>> and all the birds of the air had fled.
> I looked, and lo, the fruitful land was a desert,
>> and all its cities were laid in ruins
>> before the LORD, before his fierce anger. (Jer. 4:23–6).

By the river sits a disconsolate group of people who obviously do not belong to that city. Their musical instruments are on the ground beside them or hung on tree-branches. Some of the wealthy inhabitants of Babylon taunt them as they pass by: "Come on, give us a tune from where you come from." The taunt is met with silence and looks of despair. Later, these feelings are expressed in what has come down to us as Psalm 137, in the words 'How could we sing the Lord's song in a strange land?'

The Babylonian exile was an event that has shaped the self-awareness and self-identity of the Jewish people and the Jewish faith to this day. At the time, it was experienced not simply as the physical destruction of buildings and property, the loss of home and the bitterness of exile. More than that, it called into question the community's most deeply held beliefs about the nature of God, and about what being the chosen people might mean. They wondered whether they had disobeyed God to the extent that God's covenant with them had been broken for ever. After all, it was fundamental to their self-image that they had been delivered by their God from the slavery of Egypt and had been led into the promised land where they would live safely under God's protection for all time. The Jerusalem Temple was where God dwelt, but that now lay in ruins. How could they sing the Lord's song in a strange land?

Working in a hospice I was privileged to witness how a few people, occasionally even a young mother, could pass through the deep trauma of facing almost certain death in the near future, confront the loss of cherished plans and hopes, and manage to look the nothingness, the non-existence threatened by death, in the face; then, perhaps even in the midst of debilitating treatment, attain a place of peace. This is what happened to the lady I quoted in chapter 4. Her words about hospice-care teaching her the reality of love were indeed the singing of the Lord's song in a strange land.

I believe that lament is central to the process of dealing with difficulty, and indeed that for Christians it is a generally neglected area of the biblical tradition. Lament is a complex and multi-layered medium, encompassing much more than just grief. Western culture, and with it to a great extent Western Christianity, has largely lost the tradition of lament, and has therefore deprived itself of an important contributor to social adaptation and resilience.

In the context of global crisis, lament is not an individual and private activity but a corporate and public one. To consider it as that immediately shifts the focus away from climate grief as something that I have to face and cope with on my own, towards seeing it as affecting the whole community, and of each individual participating in the community's expression of grief. My own experience suggests that too many people are struggling alone with anxiety and depression about climate change, unable to express themselves freely about it to others, let alone being able participate in rituals of lament with others. The churches offer almost no help here at the moment. On the other hand, to meet other like-minded people in a safe space that would allow us to be open and honest about our deepest feelings could be enormously reassuring and affirmative.

Corporate lament, at its best, gives voice to the emotional responses of recognition, grief, hopelessness, protest, repentance, and hope; reflecting and enabling the expression of the feelings of participants. This is not a neat sequence or formula to be followed. It is a messy and gradual process of personal and public acceptance and denial, of self-examination and discovery.

Recognition and acknowledgement can be difficult and threatening undertakings. Grief about our plight and the plight of others, in this case of the whole earth and all that is in it, naturally follows once we admit to that plight. We should allow this grief to be freely acknowledged, something that also feels difficult in western culture. Hopelessness, like grief, can be difficult to own, especially for Christians. But I believe that it is widespread, although often numbed by diversionary activity or avoided by false reassurance. Hopelessness arises from a fundamental loss of meaning, represented most starkly by death. It is crucial that we do not make the mistake of thinking that hopelessness in the face of climate change is a sign of lack of faith, and therefore castigate ourselves or try to generate hope by force of will. There is ample evidence from the Scriptures that the darkness of despair is a natural response to extreme trauma. Look, for example, at Lamentations 3:16–18, where the prophet describes his response to the devastating destruction of Jerusalem. Talking of God, he says:

> He has made my teeth grind on gravel,
> and made me cower in ashes;
> my soul is bereft of peace;
> I have forgotten what happiness is;
> so I say, 'Gone is my glory,
> and all that I had hoped for from the LORD.'

Perhaps in the context of lament and climate change we should speak of desolation rather than hopelessness. Nonetheless, to find ourselves in this kind of darkness, in loss of meaning, with a sense that God has abandoned us, even that God is dead, is an important aspect of the complex process of adaptation to traumatic change. Although it is the last thing that it feels like to the sufferer, it can paradoxicallly be a sign of hope, because it is an indication that our traditional ways of understanding are dissolving. Perhaps not fully with our conscious minds we have understood that the ways in which we have found meaning in the world, the old stories by which we lived and made sense of things, are no longer true to things as they are. To use a phrase of Paul Tillich's, our myth is broken.[32] To know that, is to know the dark night of the soul, as John of the Cross understood. But it is also, strangely, to be nearer to God, precisely because it is a more truthful place.

If whole communities and societies can acknowledge that their myth is broken, then the task of constructing new communal meanings can begin. This is why communal lament is so important: it gives space for individuals who may have suffered their desolation in silence and tried to carry their burdens of perception on their own, to know that they are not alone, that others see things as they do, and thereby to find affirmation and assurance.

Lament can also be a sign of hope because it is an expression of protest, indicating not a resigned and weary acceptance of how things are, but a public cry of indignation and perhaps anger that things are not as they should be. The protest that we find in the Tanakh is often addressed to God, and I do not think that we should be reluctant, as I am often, to be indignant with God when we feel that God has treated us unfairly. If that is how we feel, we should integrate that feeling into our being: trying to suppress it and to summon up more respectful thoughts towards God is to be dishonest in the one place where we need to be truly honest, and to drop all our defences. If, with others, we can be indignant or perhaps angry with God in lament, then that is, simultaneously, a cry of hope: a reminder to God and to ourselves that the hope of the Gospel is of a world made otherwise, and that we must not settle for anything less.

How does repentance fit into lament? Repentance begins with recollection and, again, recognition—acknowledging our ways of thinking and living that have damaging consequences. *Metanoia*, the Greek word for repentance, means turning around, a complete change of mind, a radical transformation. This is the work of a lifetime, as we come slowly to see how entangled we are in unreality, and therefore how compromised are even our

---

[32] Paul Tillich, *Dynamics of Faith* (Harper Torchbook, 1957), 51–7.

best intentions. Particularly with climate change it is hard, truly, to admit our individual and corporate responsibility for the destruction that we have brought upon ourselves and the world. To lament at the foot of the Cross is both to acknowledge what we have done and, at the same time, to know that the fact that God suffers with us is ultimately a sign of acceptance and hope.

From the place of lament, if it is doing its work as it should be, we are better able to go out with this characteristic but distinct mingling of acceptance and hope. Acceptance that, yes, this is how it is: our lives are changing for ever and there can be no going back. Hope that says, at the same time, that a better world is possible, even in a place of desolation from which we can presently see no escape.

Coming to terms with the loss of the world that we have known is now, and will be, a complex and difficult process, possibly involving much anguish. But in our own depths, deeper than the depth of our immediate experience, we carry the suffering, death and resurrection of Jesus. Those strange events recorded in the Gospels are a model and a revelation of the pattern of creation and for our own lives. The Christian vocation, the vocation of the creation as a whole is not without cost, does not take us to the place of peace and new life without first passing through the valley of the shadow of death. When James and John asked Jesus for the best places in heaven, he could give them no such undertaking: instead, he asked them if they could drink the cup of suffering as he was about to do (Mark 10:35–7). St Paul reminds us that we have been baptized into the death of Jesus as a prerequisite of resurrection: 'Do you not know that all of us who have been baptized into Christ Jesus were baptized into his death?' (Rom. 6:3)

In *The Prophetic Imagination*, the theologian Walter Brueggemann discusses the authentic Christian life rather than climate change, but his words sum up much of what I have tried to express here about grief. Speaking of Jesus's reassurance, 'Blessed are you who weep now, for you will laugh.' (Luke 6:21), Brueggemann writes:

> There is grief work to be done in the present that the future may come. There is mourning to be done for those who do not know the deathliness of their situation. There is mourning to be done with those who know pain and suffering and lack the power or freedom to bring it to speech. The saying is a harsh one, for it sets this grief work as the precondition of joy. It announces that those who have not cared enough to grieve will not know joy.[33]

Where then can the God of *hesed*, of love and compassion, be found? For people of faith what should be the narrative and the vocation?

---

[33] Walter Brueggemann, *The Prophetic Imagination* (Fortress Press, 1978), 119.

10
VOCATION IN THE ANTHROPOCENE, THE NEW NARRATIVE

We need a radically different God from the one that an earlier age discerned. A radically different God, but a truer one, truer to the world and to the cosmos, to a universe of which we now have a much greater understanding than Kepler or Newton could have dreamed. If we take creation seriously we should, of course, put it the other way around as well: compared to earlier generations we are now living in a radically different universe that is truer to God as God really is.

How, as Christians, should we seek to live in the Anthropocene? We have seen why many of the narratives in which we have trusted are no longer adequate and how threatening this can be to our sense of who we are and of our position in the world. How, from here, do we discern and follow our vocation?

Traditionally, it is baptism that is the sign of membership of the body of Christ and the commencement of the journey of discipleship. The annual renewal of baptismal vows, or similar rites such as the Methodist covenant service, are a way of re-committing ourselves to our calling and an opportunity to reflect on how that calling is expressed in the way that we live. Christians claim to follow the example of Jesus, the divine and human revealer of God. What aspects of God is the Spirit revealing to us now, in these times?

As technology seems to give humans ever-increasing control over their environment and, potentially, the climate, the perception of the way that God acts in the world has become one of diminishing control. During the twentieth century the idea of a 'weak' and suffering God gained ground over earlier concepts of Divine omnipotence and intervention. This was perhaps the only satisfactory way to come to terms theologically with the wholesale slaughter and destruction of the 1914–18 war when for many, especially those in the trenches, the God of whom they had been taught was nowhere to be found. The final verse of the poem 'Jesus of the Scars', written just after that war by Edward Shillito (1872–1948), a Free Church minister in England during World War I, expresses this powerfully:

> The other gods were strong; but Thou wast weak;
> They rode, but Thou didst stumble to a throne;
> But to our wounds only God's wounds can speak,
> And not a god has wounds, but Thou alone.[34]

The unspeakable horror of the Holocaust in the 1939–45 war gave further impetus to the concept of a suffering God, brought to wide attention by Jürgen Moltmann with the publication of *The Crucified God*.[35] This revised perspective has immense pastoral significance and theologically is particularly relevant to where we look for God in the climate crisis. Tim Gorringe points out that,

> … Moltmann suggests that G-d's patience and capacity for suffering is the root of G-d's creative activity in history, and, quotes Moltmann: 'it is not through supernatural interventions that G-d guides creation to its goal … it is through G-d's passion and the opening of possibilities out of G-d's suffering'.[36]

---

[34] Edward Shillito, *Jesus of the Scars and Other Poems* (Hodder and Stoughton, 1919).

[35] Jürgen Moltmann, *The Crucified God: The Cross of Christ as the Foundation and Criticism of Christian Theology* (SCM Press, 1974).

[36] Gorringe, *Keeping Time*, 133.

As we ponder the nature of our vocation in a time of un-ravelling, we are reminded that we are not redeemed out of the world but as part of it. Baptism does not signify our separation from, but our incorporation into the whole, into and not out of the created world from which so much of the time we see our-selves as distinct and apart. Our God is not to be found above it all but in the midst of the unravelling, which is the place to which the path of discipleship leads, a place of comfort and of fear, of security and of profound insecurity.

Moltmann's phrase about God guiding creation to its goal is another reminder of the dynamism of the cosmos, its ceaseless change. The old, pre-evolutionary concept was that all creatures, all life, had remained unchanged since created by God in the be-ginning. This sat comfortably with a God who might intervene miraculously but who was essentially detached, a God in whom human passions had no analogy. Our current scientific knowledge prompts a very different story. It is that we humans, together with all other living things, and indeed the rest of the cosmos, are on a journey together with God into an open future. We have genuine agency, and the awful lesson of the Anthropocene is that the future survival of human and many other forms life on earth is inescap-ably in our hands. Counter-intuitively in this crisis we are called primarily not to control but to love, with the suffering that love al-ways risks. Despite our darkness and uncertainties, our faith—of which we might, in the circumstances, have no emotional reassur-ance or resonance with at all—tells us that the strange and often apparently weak and helpless power of love formed the cosmos and somehow will be the means of its fulfilment. Our choices, our actions, can help or hinder that fulfilment. The flicker of the butter-fly's wings can have momentous consequences.

This is the counter-narrative that Christianity brings to the world, the counter-narrative of God's *hesed*, built in to creation from the beginning. This is God's nature, this love that we, in our arrogance, call powerlessness, and which we see supremely in Jesus the powerless victim on the Cross. When we sometimes talk of God working at the 'margins of society', we can forget that these are *our* margins, not God's. As Jesus points out so clearly in Matthew 25, it is the victims and those with the wounds who bear the wounds of God:

> When the Son of Man comes in his glory, and all the angels with him, then he will sit on the throne of his glory. All the nations will be gathered before him, and he will separate people one from another as a shepherd separates the sheep from the goats, and he will put the sheep at his right hand and the goats at the left. Then the king will say to those at his right hand, "Come, you that are blessed by my Father, inherit the kingdom prepared for you from the foundation of the world; for I was hungry and you gave me food, I was thirsty and you gave me something to drink, I was a stranger and you welcomed me, I was naked and you gave me clothing, I was sick and you took care of me, I was in prison and you visited me." Then the righteous will answer him, "Lord, when was it that we saw you hungry and gave you food, or thirsty and gave you something to drink? And when was it that we saw you a stranger and welcomed you, or naked and gave you clothing? And when was it that we saw you sick or in prison and visited you?" And the king will answer them, "Truly I tell you, just as you did it to one of the least of these who are members of my family, you did it to me." (Matt. 25:31–40)

This is where God is to be found, this the centre of God's attention. The extent of our concern for despised victims—not just other humans, but all living beings devalued, ignored or exploited—is the measure of our alignment with the divine *hesed*. There God awaits our engagement. Placing love and justice towards the excluded at the centre of concern may be marginal to the world's economic and political agenda, but it is crucial for humanity's survival within the ecosphere.

11
BEYOND NARRATIVE
AN ECOLOGY OF THE HEART

I have described how the shock of a terminal illness could lead to the discovery of love and an entirely different perspective on life. I looked at this from the point of view of the new and healing narrative which then unfolded. Acknowledgment and acceptance of the terrifying reality of a rapidly-changing climate and environment is an essential first step towards the necessary abandonment of our old securities. Loss of narrative, and thus of meaning, is deeply threatening, and this loss takes us into a place of darkness, of unknowing. What might this darkness itself teach us?

If we manage to relinquish an inadequate narrative, then a normal response is to seek to fill the vacuum immediately with a new story. Psychologically we have to do this if we are not to lose our orientation entirely. Even in the tragedy of someone with dementia we can see that, as the old narratives of identity and personal history are lost, they are replaced by others, often completely out of touch with 'reality', through which the mind constructs stories that seek to make sense of circumstances that, to the sufferer, are unfamiliar and incomprehensible. In the context of the climate change threat—and other trauma too—even to respond with utter despair is to adopt a new narrative, albeit one that can be corrosive and destructive. If, though, we see and especially *feel* no hope, what can we do? It is not possible to embrace a new narrative of hope with integrity, and to live by it, unless we really believe in it; belief of that sort cannot be achieved through willpower, as we are aware if we are rigorous in the pursuit of self-knowledge and in the questioning of our own motivation. Something beyond the conscious mind has to shift; something in the heart, before we are able to see things anew.

Writers and teachers in the Christian contemplative tradition, and indeed in the parallel traditions of other faiths, have a consistent message: in seeking to open ourselves to the truth beyond ourselves, it is beyond our selves that we have to go. The practice of ascesis that was so prominent in the early centuries of the Church and throughout the medieval period was aimed at least in part at quelling the insistent clamour of the ego, as we would put it nowadays. In the sixteenth century, John of the Cross recognized and expressed clearly that an asceticism forced upon us by circumstance may have the potential to bear fruit in the same way as a chosen discipline of denial. If it is to come about in this way, though, the painful business of 'dying to self' cannot be sidestepped. The threatening darkness, the abyss of loss of meaning, must be acknowledged, faced as far as it can be, and accepted. There is a mystery in why suffering crushes some people totally and cruelly, when for others it prompts a shift in the heart, re-orientation and the beginning of a healing process. In response to this there can be no adequate answer, except perhaps to feel our way towards the possibility that the God with wounds, as John Taylor claimed, is also asking for our forgiveness, as we seek that of God.[37]

It has been the genius of the Christian contemplative tradition not only to recognize, but also to witness to the pattern of Christ's Passion within encounters with extreme suffering. It is this that can bring hope beyond hope, trust beyond trust. A descent into hell can become the strange gift of participation in the

---

[37] John V. Taylor, *The Christlike God* (SCM Press, 1992), 204–5.

redemptive suffering of Jesus. This, too, is mystery, and we must recognize again that the descent into hell is often just that. There may be no signposts to the other side, no shreds of assurance or comfort; only the same cry of dereliction that, according to Mark, came from the lips of Jesus on the point of death.

Such depth of suffering is not, of course, the experience of everyone, and life for many has long periods of calm and happiness. Nonetheless the pattern sketched here gives orientation to those who desire to align their lives, as far as they can, with the life of Christ and God's creation; to discern and participate in the redemptive, creative direction of the cosmos. There is an inner ascesis to which we are called even when not compelled by circumstance, one that must be impelled by love seeking love, the Spirit at work: our love reaching out towards the Divine Love, so that we come to see that what we call our love has its source in, and indeed at its purest is none other than, the Divine Love at the deepest centre of all that is made.

The aim and goal of a Christian inner ascesis is the transcendence, not the elimination, of personal subjectivity. Expressing it in these terms rather than those of the 'putting to death of the ego' is preferable for a number of reasons. Firstly, it avoids the self-violence and repression that can so easily follow from a misunderstanding of the older term. Secondly, to transcend is to go beyond limits. It indicates the inclusion of the earlier stage or state in the new, wider one, rather than its abolition. 'Union with God' has never, in Christian understanding, signified ultimate absorption into the Godhead and the disappearance of self. A continuing but transformed and fulfilled existence as persons is what we are promised. This implies a trajectory of creative development throughout life and beyond, rather than the model of painstakingly building an adequate sense of self during the first half of life only to have to dismantle it in the second half.

Thirdly, and more directly relevant to our theme, the transcendence of our subjectivity involves a profound change in how we perceive ourselves in relation to everything beyond the centre of our self-consciousness. This is Martin Buber's 'I-Thou' relationship, where the other is acknowledged and known in its own discrete subjectivity and independence.[38] Such acknowledgment must begin even with our own bodies, as Jürgen Moltmann points out:

> The alienation of the human being from his bodily existence must be viewed as the inner aspect of the external ecological crisis of modern industrial society. Religion and upbringing made people identify themselves as the subject merely of cognition and will; their bodily existence was something that had to be objectified and subdued ... Unless the person's own physical nature is liberated from its subjugation by the subject, nature in the environmental sense will not be liberated from the estrangement brought about by the subjection and exploitation imposed upon it.[39]

This is a strong claim, but it can be seen how it aligns with our analysis of end-of-life care at its best. To allow the clinical narrative to dominate in a terminal illness cannot promote the acceptance and healing that may lead to a more peaceful dying: to do so is to subjugate the 'physical nature' in the name of control, a control that will, in these circumstances, inevitably fail. In the same way, to put our hope for the future of the earth in the clinical narrative of technological control is to maintain the attitude of dominance that has brought us to this point of crisis.

---

[38] Martin Buber, *I and Thou*, trans. by Ronald Gregor Smith (Charles Scribner's Sons, 1958), 26. Buber asserts that the 'I-Thou' relationship is a direct interpersonal relationship that is not mediated by any intervening system of ideas. Thus, 'I-Thou' is not a means to some object or goal, but is a relationship involving the whole being of each subject.

[39] Jürgen Moltmann, *God in Creation: An Ecological Doctrine of Creation*, The Gifford Lectures 1984–1985 (SCM Press, 1985), 48–9.

To recognize the 'Thou' of whatever is other to us, starting with our own bodies and extending from there to other people and to the whole of 'nature' is the path of contemporary ascesis. To find a safe space in the fear, radical uncertainty and insecurity of the Anthropocene is not to live without story—we cannot do that—but without the ownership and appropriation of any narrative. If we can begin to transcend our subjectivity, so too will we start to transcend the narratives to which we cling for our self-definition. In the swirl of stories about what the future will be like it is unwise either to rely for our sense of security and our hope on any of the more optimistic outlooks, or to give way to despair if we believe the forecasts of the doom-sayers. The new narrative by which to live should be one of detachment, to the extent that we can attain that. The last thing that detachment means in this context is an uninvolved and unengaged attitude of superiority or cynicism. Rather it refers precisely to the disengagement of the ego from having a stake in any particular story or ideology. This includes detachment at an ever-deeper level, including from what we call our faith, in so far as we think of that as something that we possess and therefore can lose. Any faith that we think of as ours can so easily obstruct a clear view of the truth. Our trust is in the faith of Christ, not in *our* faith in Christ.

To find and inhabit a story that can bear the burden of meaning of the Anthropocene involves learning to sit lightly with all and any narratives, while that meaning and our future is still dark to us. This is a new pastoral narrative, or rather an old one that has become urgently relevant: the narrative of darkness, of a real unknowing, of a stripping and an undoing of kenosis. This is a detachment that liberates both for action and for love. For action, because our agenda is not skewed in our own selfish direction, but as far as possible is inclusive of the good of the whole. For love, because the ego, with its self-regard, no longer stands in the way of genuine openness to the Thou, the Thou of God and the Thou of those we love, the Thou of our neighbour and of the whole created order, with all the vulnerability and risk that entails.

Our baptism into the world is, as was that of Jesus, an act of subversion, and is thus inescapably political. It is subversive because it is a public demonstration of our refusal to identify with the dominant narrative of our times, because by it we dare to claim that the social nomos is holding us in thrall to the false gods of our own projection. It is political because it stands as a challenge to the current power structures, and as such can be expected to attract condemnation and opposition to the extent that we are true to our vocation.

Most of us can only hope to make a beginning upon the journey initiated at baptism. But even as we do so we will find ourselves walking alongside Jesus, both as He sets his face towards the Passion at Jerusalem, and also in the as-yet-unfulfilled eschaton of the Emmaus road. To learn to live in this way, beyond narrative, is to live the paradox of a joyful dying. Dying, because of our mortality and the death of so much that is good in our generation. Joyful, because of the sheer generosity of lived experience moment by moment, in all its beauty, pain and mystery. This is the place for lament and for praise, where we become, in ourselves and in our daily lives and actions, the intercession, the working and the yearning for a world made otherwise, for the transformation of suffering and the revealing of the liberation of the Divine Realm.

SLG PRESS PUBLICATIONS

slgpress.co.uk